CAROL

C000050809

Pisa

MICHELIN
Travel Publications

CONTENTS

Pisa has the atmosphere of a minor capital city which has lost some of its hustle and bustle. Its superb buildings reflect past splendours. The city is more spacious than Florence and less austere thanks to its yellow, pink or yellow-ochre house fronts but, like Florence, it is bisected by the River Arno, which forms one of its most majestic meanders at this point.

All this splendour is eclipsed, however, by the delicate glory of the buildings in the famous Piazza, which is aptly known as Miracles Square. ■

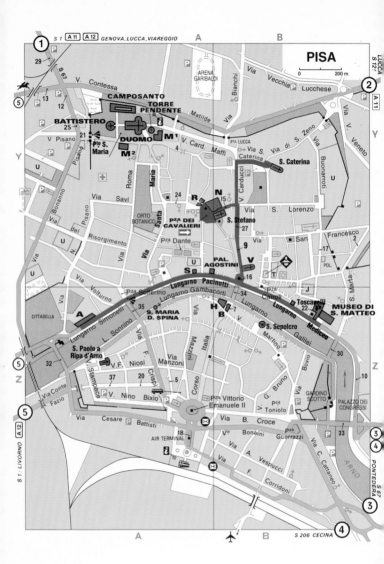

PISA

0 ——— 200 m

Location

Population 92 379. Pisa is located near the mouth of the Arno but separated from the sea by the Migliarino-San Rossore-Massaciùccoli Park.
🚩 *Piazza dei Miracoli, 56126 Pise,* ☎ *050 56 04 64.*

MARITIME SPLENDOUR

When it was founded c 7C BC, Pisa was on the coast but the shoreline soon receded some distance from the city because of the accumulation of alluvium at the mouth of the Arno; this development can be seen in the plain extending westwards from the city and in the flat seabed. The city was occupied by the Etruscans and was an ally of Rome for many years. From 180 BC onwards it was colonised by the Romans who took advantage of its geographical location on the banks of the Arno only a few miles from the sea and turned it into a naval base free from the risk of attack by pirates. Pisa continued to fulfil the role of a naval base until the fall of the Roman Empire in the West in AD 476.

In AD 888 the city became an independent republic but not until the Middle Ages did it begin to take advantage of its geographical location to encourage economic development. Like Genoa and Venice, the city was one of the powerful maritime republics which resisted the Muslim domination; its "merchant-warriors" fought stubbornly throughout the Mediterranean Basin. Pisa took possession of Sardinia in 1015 and later of Corsica, over which it exercised absolute control in

H. Ayeva/MICHELIN

the last quarter of the 11C. In 1114 it captured the Balearic Islands. It expanded its conquests into Tunisia and began to set up trading posts in the eastern part of the Mediterranean, which extended as far as Syria.

Pisa developed into a very active port in the 11C and reached the peak of its prosperity in the 12C and first half of the 13C. Its ships plied the Mediterranean carrying arms, wool, furs, leather and timber from the Apennines to the Orient, together with iron mined on the Isle of Elba. They returned with spices, silk and cotton. This period was marked by the construction of the finest buildings and the founding of the university, which still enjoys a reputation for excellence.

When a major quarrel, the Investiture Controversy, broke out between the Papacy and the Empire in the late 11C, Pisa, a resolutely Ghibelline city, rallied to the Emperor's camp. At sea it successfully resisted the threat of Genoa, its main maritime rival for commercial supremacy in the Mediterranean. On land it withstood its two Guelf rivals, Lucca and Florence.

When Pisa was deprived of the support of Emperor Frederick II (d 1250) and of King Manfred, his son who was killed in 1266, the city began to fall into decline. In August 1284 at the great **Battle of Meloria** the Pisan fleet was wiped out by Genoese ships. The city was forced to transfer all its rights in Corsica to Genoa and to give up Sardinia. It was unable to prevent the collapse of its commercial empire in the East as it was cut off from its trading posts by the loss of its fleet. The city was also undermined by internal strife and was eventually taken over by Florence in 1406.

Lorenzo the Magnificent (Medici dynasty) reorganised its university and began to build a new one. In the 16C Pisa was incorporated into the Grand Duchy of Tuscany and Cosimo I founded the Order of the **Knights of St Stephen** in the city. During this period the city enjoyed a renewal of its influence, mainly in the sciences. ∎

PISAN ART

Between the 11C and the 13C, while the city was increasing in economic prosperity and political power, an innovative art form was developing that had a marked effect on architecture and sculpture.

■ Religious Architecture

This type of architecture, which was different from the other styles present in Italy during the Romanesque period, reached its heyday in the 13C and spread throughout Tuscany, to towns such as Lucca, Pistoia and Arezzo. It also left its mark on churches in Sardinia and Corsica, both then Pisan possessions.

The style was known as **Pisan Romanesque** and it brought together a pleasing combination of several influences, most markedly the architecture of Lombardy. To it was added a wealth of decoration inspired by the shapes and motifs of articles brought back from the Orient or the Islamic world by the Pisan fleet. This trend led to buildings of outstanding elegance and unity of which the cathedral in Pisa is the most rigorous and solemn example. The west front, side walls and apse are all skilfully faced with green and white marble, a costly building material that was as popular in Pisa as it was in

H. Ayeva/MICHELIN

10

other Tuscan towns, in particular Florence. Whereas the architects of Florence emphasised the geometric divisions on the façades of churches by framing them in marble, the craftsmen of Pisa made extensive use of relief – tall but shallow blind arcading running all round the building and galleries with colonnettes, a feature that is discreetly present in Lombard architecture but used in Pisa with great exuberance, marking off the upper section of the gable and dappling it with light and shade. Rose windows, diamond shapes and other small motifs picked out in marble marquetry show Oriental inspiration in their use of colour.

In the second half of the 11C and early 12C the architects whose names are inextricably linked with the great buildings of Pisa were **Buscheto, Rainaldo** his direct successor who was a contemporary of **Diotisalvi**, and **Bonanno Pisano**, architect and sculptor. **Giovanni di Simone** was the main architect working in the second half of the 13C.

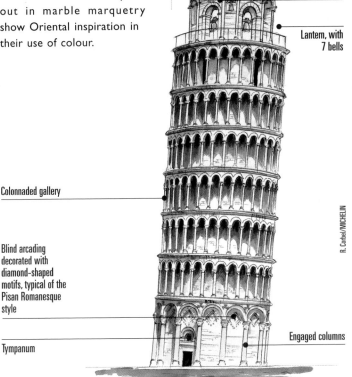

Arcatures

Lantern, with 7 bells

Colonnaded gallery

Blind arcading decorated with diamond-shaped motifs, typical of the Pisan Romanesque style

Tympanum

Engaged columns

■ Pisan Sculpture in the 13C and 14C

Local artists such as **Bonanno Pisano** and **Fra' Guglielmo**, or Lombards such as Guido da Como, worked on the decoration of the Romanesque churches of Pisa in the 12C and early 13C. It was, however, Nicola Pisano, a sculptor thought to have come from Apulia, who is credited with paving the way for a whole succession of artists in the second half of the 13C. In their eyes Pisa was the birthplace of Italian Romanesque and especially of Gothic sculpture.

These sculptors, who were also architects and interior decorators, were responsible for the creation of huge and unusual pulpits, veritable masterpieces owing to their harmonious structure, their intricate decoration and the aesthetic beauty of their carvings.

Nicola Pisano (born c 1220, died shortly after 1280) had studied classical sculpture. He assimilated its majesty and power but added to it the sense of humanity and the realism

seen in the paintings of his contemporary, Giotto. His main works are the pulpit in the Baptistery in Pisa and in the cathedral in Siena. With the assistance of his son, Giovanni, who worked with him in Siena, he also built the Fontana Maggiore in Perugia. One of his pupils was Arnolfo di Cambio, the architect of the cathedral in Florence.

Giovanni Pisano (born c 1250, died c 1315-20) was undoubtedly the greatest of all the sculptors. He had a more flexible technique and was more concerned with the expression of dramatic intensity. He worked with his father until the latter's death. His art form developed towards the creation of compositions that were increasingly complex with figures that were more and more tormented, although they were also filled with an outstanding intensity, which gave them a wonderful life-

Ph. Orain/MICHELIN

like quality. It was his genius that created the splendid pulpit in the Siena cathedral and in Sant'Andrea in Pistoia. He was also the first person to direct work on Siena cathedral, which he wanted to cover with huge statues like the Gothic cathedrals in France which he had visited c 1270. Giovanni was the last member of the first Pisano dynasty and his death marked the end of the great period of powerful and monumental Gothic sculptures in Tuscany. His most able pupil was Tino di Camaino, from Siena.

Andrea da Pontedera, named after a town near Pisa and also known as **Andrea Pisano**, was born at the end of the 13C and worked mainly in Florence where one

of his major works was the first bronze door for the Baptistery. His elegant and refined style, which he developed while training as a goldsmith, and his attractively-drawn scenes were not inspired by his Pisan predecessors. He also sculpted some powerful high reliefs used to decorate the bell tower by Giotto in Florence.

Andrea's son, **Nino Pisano**, who died c 1365-70, preferred to work in the round. He was a past master in the art of relief and he created graceful Madonnas including a famous *Madonna del Latte* (in the San Matteo National Museum). This second Pisano dynasty, which also included **Tommaso**, Nino's brother, enjoyed a reputation in the late 14C that made their workshop an obligatory training ground for a number of great Sienese and Florentine sculptors in the early 15C, including Lorenzo Ghiberti and Jacopo della Quercia. ■

PISAN FESTIVALS

■ Historical Regatta of the Maritime Republics (May/June)

Since 1956 the Regatta of the Four Maritime Republics (Amalfi, Genoa, Venice and Pisa) has been held in each city in turn. The festivities begin with a costumed pageant. The procession makes its way through the city, together with historical figures: Kinzica de' Sismondi, dressed all in pink, the heroine whose courage saved Pisa when it was besieged by the Saracens; the Duke of Amalfi in a gold costume; Guglielmo Embriaco from Genoa, also known as Testa di Maglio; the Doge of Venice accompanied by Caterina Cornaro. The regatta itself is a boat race in which the old rival republics compete.

■ The "Luminara" of San Ranieri (16 June)

On the evening before the Feast Day of St Rainier the patron saint of the city, the Lungarno Mediceo and Lungarno Galilei quays are lit with hundreds of tiny lanterns outlining the windows, architectural lines of mansions, parapets along the quays and the architecture of Santa Maria della Spina. The lanterns are reflected in the Arno where other tiny lights float on the water. This festival of light is best seen at sunset. After nightfall there is a spectacular firework display.

■ Historic Regatta in Honour of San Ranieri (17 June)

In the afternoon a regatta is held on the Arno, using historic boats. Four of the city's historical districts (*Rioni*) compete against each other in a race (2km/1mi) against the

The banks of the Arno are a favourite venue for festivals and celebrations

Gronchi Fotoarte

current; the rowers are dressed in traditional costume.

■ Il Gioco del Ponte (last Sunday in June)

Based on the game of *mazzascudo* played at least as far back as the 12C, the *Gioco del Ponte* is said to have been played for the first time on 22 February 1569. The Pisans have always been very proud of their game and they would not permit it to be copied in any of the territories they conquered, as shown in a decree dated 1318 concerning Sardinia. The various districts of the town are organised in two groups reflecting the two parts of the city which is divided by the Arno – the north bank *(Tramontana)* and the south bank *(Mezzogiorno)*. They compete on the Middle Bridge *(Ponte di Mezzo)*, which is divided into two equal sections where the teams take up their positions. The aim is to gain control of the entire bridge. Over the centuries the rules have remained unchanged but the game has been altered to make it less violent. The *Mazzascudo,* literally a bludgeon-shield, had one narrow end designed for attack and one broad end for defence. For the game it was

replaced by a limewood or poplar shield *(targone)*, which had more or less the same shape, that of a small oar, but was less dangerous. Nevertheless the hand-to-hand struggles between men in armour continued to be violent and so, since the Second World War, the competition has consisted of pushing the other team backwards across the bridge using a 7-tonne cart mounted on a central rail. A flag drops automatically as soon as the entire cart has crossed into the other camp. The sixdistricts in each of the two halves of the city compete against each other in groups of two. The overall winner is the team which has obtained at least four victories in the quarter- and semi-finals.

Before the game the two "armies", each bearing their local colours, parade along the quaysides in two processions of more than 300 people dressed in ornate 16C costumes and armour. The procession of magistrates, which has some 60 participants, is separate and neutral. On the following Sunday the pennant *(palio)* is formally handed over to the winning team in the Palazzo Comunale. Festivities are then held in the victorious districts. ■

HIGHLIGHTS

PIAZZA DEI MIRACOLI★★★

Allow 3hr.

This prestigious square, which is also known as **Piazza del Duomo** (Cathedral Square), contains four buildings which constitute one of the most famous sight in the world.

It resembles a vast enclosure, lined on two sides by a slim wall of red brick to which crenellations were added in the mid-12C. Within are the dazzling white marble mass of the baptistery and the cathedral

with its famous bell tower, known as the Leaning Tower of Pisa. In the background is the cemetery (Camposanto) with its long row of blind arcading, also made of white marble.

This succession of buildings is best seen from **Porta Santa Maria** and it is also from this point that the angle of the Leaning Tower is most spectacular. ∎

TORRE PENDENTE***

The **Leaning Tower of Pisa** (58m/189ft high) is the symbol of the city. The architect did not intend the tower to lean. Its angle is caused by the alluvial soil, which is not compact enough to bear the weight of the building.

The building work was begun by **Bonanno Pisano** in 1173 and had reached the first floor when the first subsidence occurred. The architect, however, ignored it and another two storeys were built. When the second subsidence occurred, work stopped and did not start again until a century later when another architect, Giovanni di Simone, tried to correct the angle of slope by ensuring that the side which was sinking into the ground carried less weight. He died at the Battle of Meloria before his work was completed. The top of the bell tower was added in 1350.

The peculiarity of the tower cannot conceal the beauty of its architecture. It was built as a cylinder, like the towers in Byzantium, and has six floors of galleries which seem, because of the angle of incline, to be unwinding in an ethereal spiral. On the lower level, in the purest of Pisan Romanesque styles, is the circle of blind arcading decorated with diamond-shaped motifs. ■

A Prestigious Landmark

Since 1178, when the tower was first observed to lean, over 8 000 projects have been drawn up to remedy the problem, with varying degrees of success. From 1550 to 1817, the leaning process was stopped owing to reinforcement works carried out by Vasari. Unfortunately, in the 19C, hydraulic engineers modified the soil structure by pumping the water table. The tower was closed to the public on 7 January 1990 because of the inherent danger of collapse and has incurred constant remedial work.

– two stainless steels rings were placed around the first floor.

– In 1991, the tower was attached to the ground by 18 steel cables.

– in 1993, the foundations were strengthened with a reinforced concrete sheath containing 670 tonnes of lead (1m/3.28ft in length) to counterbalance the lean.

– Early in 1994, it was noted that the tower had moved back towards the vertical by 9mm/0.036in.

– In December 1998, steel-cable "braces" were attached to the tower, then removed in 2001.

The gradient has been reduced by 45cm/1.4ft. The 294 steps can be climbed again, and from the top there is a superb view⋆ of the square and the city spread out below. In fine weather the view extends across the countryside to the coast. In this prestigious university town, however, it is worth recalling the age-old curse that is so well known to Italians – "Any student hoping to graduate should never risk the climb to the top."

DUOMO ★★

The two architects of the cathedral were Buscheto (1063) and Rainaldo, who completed it towards the middle of the 12C after enlarging the transept and extending the nave towards the west front which he also designed.

It was the fabulous booty brought back to the city after major victories over the Saracens in Sicily that provided the funds required for its construction. Pisa Cathedral is a vast building in the shape of a Latin Cross and it gives an impression of being wonderfully well-balanced with its long nave, huge transept and boldly-projecting apse. To counterbalance this solemnity, a light touch is created by the rows of galleries on the west front, the blind arcading, the three rows of windows flanked by pilasters round the building and the bonding with alter-

nating light and dark marble stringcourses. All these features formed the major characteristics of the Pisan Romanesque style.

Set in the **west front***** decorated with elegant geometric motifs picked out in marquetry and mosaics of marble and multicoloured glazed terracotta is the tomb of Buscheto (*first arch on the left*). Bronze **doors*** cast in 1602 to designs by Giambologna replaced the original doors which were destroyed by fire in the late 16C. They depict the Life of the Virgin Mary (*centre*) and the Life of Christ (*sides*).

The most famous of the doors is the one named San Ranieri, which opens into the south transept opposite the Leaning Tower. Its admirable Romanesque bronze **panels**** were cast in the late 12C and designed by Bonanno Pisano. Using a rigorous economy of figures but showing prodigious inventiveness, he depicted the Life of Christ in 20 small tableaux in a manner that was highly stylised and gracefully.

Galileo

Galileo Galilei was born in 1564 into a well-educated family in Pisa. He abandoned his medical studies in favour of physics and astronomy. He was only 19 when, watching a swinging lamp in the cathedral in his native town, he realised that the oscillations always took the same amount of time whatever their range. From this observation he developed the principle of the pendulum and decided to apply the measurement of its movement to the measurement of time. He used the Leaning Tower of Pisa to study the laws of falling bodies and uniformly accelerated motion. In the field of optics he built one of the very earliest microscopes.

■ Interior

The interior of the building is less uniform than the exterior. It is a very impressive sight with its nave (100m/325ft long), five aisles, deep apse, triple-bay transept and slightly oval dome. The 68 columns, each carved out of a single block of stone, provide an amazing variety of perspectives. The overall effect of lightness created by the upper galleries for women opening onto the nave and transept and by the alternating light and dark bands of colour along the upper section of the building is somewhat muted by the gilded wooden coffering that has replaced the original coffered ceiling, which was destroyed by fire. The painted decoration on the arches in the chancel has the same muting effect.

The mosaic of *Christ Pantocrator* on the vaulting above the apse dates from the early 14C. The head of St John the Evangelist is by Cimabue, while the angel musicians under the arch are by Ghirlandaio. The splendid **pulpit★★★** on which **Giovanni Pisano** worked for almost ten years (1302-11) is a masterpiece of strength and delicacy.

The pulpit itself is supported by porphyry columns, two of which stand on lions, a motif taken from the Lombard tradition, and by five pillars decorated with statues. The female figures on the central pillar symbolise the theological virtues – Faith, Hope and Charity. The pillar stands on a base decorated with small figures representing the Liberal Arts.

On the pillars round the edge of the pulpit *(from left to right starting on the side facing the chancel)* the carvings represent St Michael, the Evangelists carrying Christ, the cardinal virtues – Fortitude, Justice, Prudence and Temperance –

supporting a woman with a baby at her breast, an allegorical representation of the Church being nourished by the Old and New Testaments, and Hercules.

The pulpit is almost circular owing to the eight slightly-convex carved panels. In a set of tumultuous carvings filled with human figures Giovanni Pisano gave full vent to his talent for expressiveness and his sense of the dramatic. The first panel *(from left to right starting at the entrance to the pulpit)* depicts the Annunciation and the Visitation of the Virgin Mary, followed by the Nativity, the Adoration of the Magi, the Presentation in the Temple and the Flight into Egypt, the Massacre of the Innocents, Christ's Passion, the Crucifixion and the Last Judgement *(two panels)*.

Near the pulpit is the bronze lamp, known as Galileo's Lamp. According to tradition it was while watching the lamp swing as it was lit by the sexton that Galileo was inspired to develop his famous theory. In fact Galileo had already made his discovery a few years before the lamp was placed in the cathedral.

The Crucifix above the high altar was made by Giambologna who also created the two bronze angel candlesticks at the corners of the choir screen. Two 16C paintings face each other on pillars on each side of the chancel – *(right) St Agnes* by Andrea del Sarto and *(left)* a *Madonna and Child* by Antonio Sogliani. ■

Top left corner: coffered ceiling in the Duomo

Below: detail of the pulpit by Giovanni Pisano

Ph. Orain/MICHELIN

BATTISTERO***
(BAPTISTERY)

This is a majestic, circular building almost equal to the height of the Leaning Tower. It took 250 years to build. Work began in 1153, almost a century after building commenced on the cathedral, and lasted, with a break of 50 years in the 13C, until 1400. The project and the early work were directed by Diotisalvi. Nicola and Giovanni Pisano also worked on the Baptistery, producing many of the carvings and sculptures.

Like the blind arcading and colonnaded galleries in the bell tower, the external decoration of the Baptistery was designed to reflect the ornamentation on the cathedral. Although the first two levels were designed in the Pisan Romanesque style, there is a decidedly Gothic flavour about the second floor and the gables and pinnacles above the arches on the first floor. At the very top of the building is a strange dome rising to a small, truncated pyramid and a statue of St John the Baptist.

The doors are among the most decorative features in the building. The one opposite the cathedral, the most ornate of the four, is flanked by columns carved with foliage in the 13C. On the lintel, carved in a Byzantine style, are episodes from the Life of St John the Baptist; above is a representation of Jesus between the Virgin Mary and St John with the four Evangelists on either side, alternating with angels. On the jambs

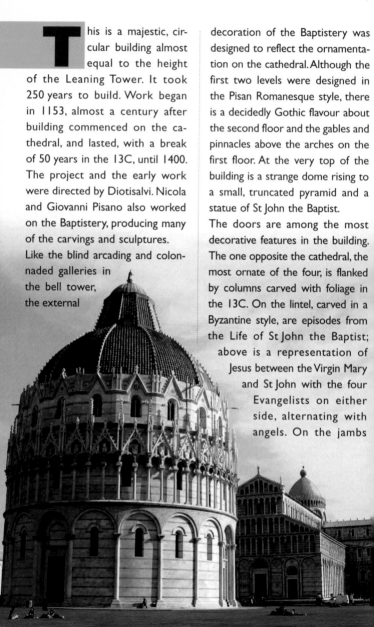

are illustrations of the work of the 12 months of the year *(left)* and carvings of the apostles (right).

■ Interior

The interior (35m/114ft in diameter) is impressive for its tall rows of arcading and its deep dome. The alternating strips of light and dark marble create an austere form of decoration. Elegant monolithic columns with attractively-carved capitals alternate with huge pillars to form a uniform peristyle on the lower level with a wide gallery above which is open to visitors *(staircase left of the entrance)*. The effect of the near-perfect spatial layout can be seen at its best from the gallery. The circular building, articulated by the ring of columns and pillars, converges on the superb octagonal **font★**, austere in its design, which is repeated in the paving and on the ground towards the outside like an echo. It was designed in 1246 by Guido Bigarelli, an artist from Como. Against the interior wall are small cylindrical basins in which newborn babies were immersed. The tank is slightly raised and decorated with square marble panels containing roses carved with acanthus leaves and animal heads. There are also insets of small multi-coloured geometric motifs of Oriental design. The altar panels, which were made in the same style in the previous century, originally formed the chancel screen in the cathedral.

The Baptistery also has an admirable **pulpit★★**, carved by Nicola Pisano who completed it in 1260. It is more austere than the one produced for the cathedral and it stands on plain columns. Semicircular arches, in which the trefoil design nevertheless points to the imminence of the Gothic style, support the pulpit which consists of five framed panels and groups of red marble columns. On one of the corners is a lectern shaped like an eagle, the emblem of St John. In retracing the Life of Christ, the artist sought inspiration in the classical sculptures seen on the Roman sarcophagi in the Camposanto. This influence is particularly strong in the first two panels *(going from left to right)* representing the Nativity and the Adoration of the Magi in which the Virgin Mary resembles a Roman matron. The following panels depict the Presentation in the Temple, the Crucifixion and the Last Judgement; the face of Lucifer *(bottom right-hand corner)* is reminiscent of the masks used in Classical theatre). ■

CAMPOSANTO ★★

The cemetery is almost as famous as the other buildings in Piazza del Duomo. Building began in 1277 under the direction of Giovanni di Simone, the second architect to work on the bell tower, but was interrupted by the war against Genoa which ended in the Battle of Meloria (1284); the cemetery was not finished until the 15C. One of the gates opening in the Romanesque blind arcading along the south wall is surmounted by a charming little Gothic construction with tracery which was added in the 14C. Inside is a statue of the *Madonna and Child* carved in the workshops of Giovanni Pisano.

Originally designed like an open air cathedral nave, this huge graveyard now resembles vast cloisters, as the tall Romanesque arches were converted in the 15C into wonderfully light four-bay Gothic windows. In the middle is the Sacred Field (*Camposanto*) which is said to have been laid out using earth brought back from Golgotha in the early 13C by the Crusaders. The earth was said to have the power to reduce dead bodies to skeletons in a few days. The galleries are paved with 600 tombstones and contain several superb Greco-Roman sarcophagi, most of them re-used in the Middle Ages for the burials of Pisan noblemen.

The walls used to be covered with admirable frescoes painted in the second half of the 14C and in the following century by artists such as Benozzo Gozzoli, Taddeo Gaddi, Andrea di Buonaiuto and Antonio Veneziano. In July 1944 artillery caused a fire which melted the lead roof, destroying or badly damaging most of the frescoes. Some of them, however, were saved and restored, including the famous fresco depicting the *Triumph of Death*, attributed to Buffalmacco, who also painted the *Last Judgement, Hell* and the *Story of the Anchorites in the Thebaid*.

Walk round the Camposanto anti-clockwise.

The Triumph of Death

St Macaire is depicted *(left)* holding an unrolled scroll and pointing to the decomposed bodies of three kings, while he explains to a group of noblemen on their way to a hunt that the only reality is death, the inevitable. Above are Anchorite monks calmly preparing for death as they go about their daily business. Death *(right)* is ignoring a group of beggars pleading for his attention *(in the centre)* and preparing instead to swoop down triumphantly on a party of carefree young people in a delightful orchard.

The scene is presented on two levels: on the hill *(left)*, ascetic life is depicted, as a token of eternal life; down the hill, is the meeting of Three Dead and Three Living Men. According to a legend known throughout Europe, three knights met three lifelike skeletons, reminding them that death is inescapable. In the Italian version, between the two groups stands the hermit (the monk Macaire in the painting), wise interpreter of the ominous meeting and life model, while the dead are represented in open tombs. A group of young people *(right)* enjoy themselves in a garden. Death is soaring above the vanity of life, and souls are taken over by angels and demons.

■ North Gallery

Beyond a small chapel, containing the St Rainier Altar carved by Tino di Camaino, is a room containing a photographic reconstruction of the frescoes as they were originally. In the centre of the room is a very fine Attic marble urn (2C BC) carved with Dionysian scenes in light relief.

Ph. Orair/MICHELIN

■ Fresco Room

The great chamber beyond contains the frescoes which have been removed from the walls in the galleries. Among them *(left wall)* is the *Triumph of Death*★★★, one of the most interesting examples of 14C Italian painting.

The two magnificent frescoes covering the end wall of the room and part of the next wall represent the *Last Judgement*★★ and *Hell*★. These were originally part of the same cycle as the previous fresco. The *Story of the Anchorites in the Thebaid (beyond)* depicts various details of the hard, lonely and ascetic life led by the early Christians who sought refuge in Egypt from persecution. On the last wall *(right of the entrance)* are *Satan's pact with God* and *The Sufferings of Job* by Taddeo Gaddi.

■ West Gallery

Against the wall are the chains that used to close off the entrance to the harbour. This gallery was the first one to be filled with the lavish tombs of Pisan noblemen from the 16C onwards. Each tomb was placed symmetrically in relation to the others. The East Gallery was organised in the same way. In the 18C the custom became so popular that the tombs began to spread into the longer North and South Galleries. In 1807 Carlo Lasinio was appointed Curator and he introduced the ancient sarcophagi which had lain along the sides of the cathedral and in the many monasteries and churches in Pisa. ■

Ph. Drain/MICHELIN

MUSEUMS

■ Museo delle Sinopie★

This museum, formerly a hospice built in the 13C and 14C, contains the underdrawings of the Camposanto frescoes.

During the restoration work on the frescoes which had been seriously damaged in 1944 the underdrawings were also removed and restored. They are now skilfully displayed in a high-ceilinged chamber covering two floors.

Ground Floor – Most of the underdrawings displayed here were sketched in the 15C and are very rough since it was customary for artists to work at their studies on paper and only the main lines of the work were sketched on the wall.

Upper Floor – A series of platforms (staircase at the end of the room) gives a panoramic view of the gigantic underdrawings created before the completion of the most famous frescoes in the Camposanto. At the end of the room is the underdrawing for the *Crucifixion,* the first fresco to be painted c 1320-30 by Francesco di Traino who was the most important artist in Pisa in the 14C. The grandiose compositions used for the *Triumph of Death,* the *Last Judgement* and *Hell* (the last two were sketched in a single session using wide sweeping lines) and the *Story of the*

Detail of frescoes in the Camposanto: the «sinopie», or underdrawings, are in the museum

Ph. Orsini/MICHELIN

Sinopia

Although frescoes can withstand the passage of time and the effects of the elements, they must be painted on a fresh base. They therefore have two main disadvantages – they have to be completed quickly and, once dry, cannot be touched up. In order to overcome these disadvantages, artists used to draw a sketch called an underdrawing *(sinopia)* on the wall, after the initial base had been prepared. This type of sketch got its name from a town, Sinope, on the shores of the Black Sea which provided the reddish-brown pigment usually used to draw them. Once the scene had been roughly sketched in, the artist could take his time to produce the final work, preparing the base only for the area he wanted to paint on a particular day. Many of these underdrawings have come to light over the past few decades as frescoes have been removed from walls for restoration.

Anchorites in the Thebaid show the remarkable drawing talents, especially in the facial expressions.

Two higher galleries provide different views of the works.

■ Museo dell'Opera del Duomo★★

The works in the museum come from the buildings in Piazza dei Miracoli. Room I gives visitors a view of the buildings, in the form of 19C models, before seeing the sculptures and furnishings.

Ground Floor – The first pulpit produced (1158 to 1162) for the cathedral *(Room 2)* was carved by Guglielmo, the architect and sculptor, who was in charge of the building work; it was his greatest master-piece. In 1310 it was replaced by the pulpit carved by Giovanni Pisano and given to Cagliari Cathedral in Sardinia. Copies of the pulpit are shown here and its structure was such that it became a prototype for future creations throughout Tuscany. The foreign works *(Room 3)* are part of the cathedral's furnishings and the shapes imported from distant lands enriched the early, mainly Classical, Romanesque architecture. Most of the additions were from the Islamic world with which the Pisans were well acquainted owing to their maritime trading links. New geometric and iconographic motifs were introduced, with a taste for polychrome marble inlay, a craft form which was already known through Byzantine art and architecture. Sculptures from Provence – a head of David – and Burgundy – a wooden statue of Christ – prove that there were links with French Romanesque artists.

The other buildings in the square – the tower *(Room 4)* and the Baptistery *(Rooms 5 and 6)* – are celebrated together with their glorious Pisan sculptures. The nine busts *(in the cloister gallery)*, which adorned the top of the Baptistery loggia, were the work (1269-79) of Nicola Pisano and his son, Giovanni Pisano. The latter also created (1302-10) the second pulpit *(Room 5)* and some other works *(Room 7)* – the *Madonna of Henry VII*, a French-inspired composition showing the Virgin Mary seated with the Child Jesus standing on her lap, and *Pisa Kneeling*, which was part of the same work completed in 1312 in honour of the Emperor. The bust of the *Madonna and Child* is a markedly Gothic work but the mute expressiveness of the eyes is typical of Giovanni's style.

The Sienese sculptor **Tino di Camaino** *(Room 8)*, who worked in Pisa for many years, was one of the most famous sculptors of funeral monuments in the 14C. The statues of the Emperor, four of his advisers, an *Annunciation* and two angels (1315) come from his mausoleum for Henry VII of Luxembourg who died in 1313.

Nino Pisano *(Room 9)* also created a number of the tombs in the cathedral in the second half of the 14C.

The tomb of Archbishop Giovanni Scherlatti so delighted Archbishop Francesco Moricotti that he asked Nino to create an identical one for him; this explains why the face on the recumbent statue is so young – he died 27 years after the sculptor. The main figure in the 15C art world was the Florentine, Andrea di Francesco Guardi *(Room 10)*, a pupil in Donatello's workshop. His main piece of work was Archbishop Pietro Ricci's tomb.

The cathedral treasury *(Room 11)* displays some of the oldest and most precious items – an 11C ivory chest decorated with *putti* and animals, a small 12C silver gilt Crucifix known as the "Pisans' Cross" (the pedestal mount dates from the 14C), two Limoges reliquaries (12C), and six fragments of the cathedral girdle *(cintola)* dating from the 13C and 14C. It was made of red damask decorated with narrative metal plaques and precious stones and, before it mysteriously disappeared, it used to be laid right round the cathedral on major feast days. There is the charming little *Madonna and Child* by Giovanni Pisano (1299) in which the curvature of the Virgin Mary's spine follows the natural curve in the elephant tusk used to carve it. The display cabinets *(Room 12)* contain pieces of silver plate made for the cathedral from the 16C to 19C – reliquaries, Crucifixes, monstrances, and chalices.

First Floor – The 15C-18C paintings and sculptures *(Rooms 13-14)* are followed by *(Room 15)* the marquetry decorating the choir stalls in the cathedral. This art form was very fashionable in the late 15C and 16C and it reveals the artists' talent in producing a sense of perspective. The three panels depicting *Faith, Hope* and *Charity* were made by Baccio and Piero Pontelli to drawings by Botticelli. The panels by Guido da Seravallino show views of the quays in Pisa in the 15C.

Among the illuminated manuscripts and antiphonies *(Room 16)* are two *"Exultet"* – one made in Benevento in the 12C, the other in Tuscany in the 13C. On one side of these rolls was a transcript of the liturgical chant sung by a deacon on Easter Saturday while on the other were the paintings seen by the congregation, representing scenes from the mystery of the Resurrection. The vestments *(Rooms 17 to 20)* provide an opportunity to admire fabrics and embroideries dating from the 15C to 19C. The display also includes Flemish lace.

The final part of the museum deals with archaeology – Egyptian, Etruscan and Roman remains collected from the various churches and monasteries in Pisa in the 19C by Carlo Lasinio, the curator of the Camposanto. With his son, he also produced a series of etchings based on the Camposanto frescoes (which unfortunately were almost completely destroyed in 1944). ■

H. Ayeva/MICHELIN

TOURS

SQUARES, CHURCHES

Once seduced by the Piazza dei Miracoli, remember to save your energies for the discovery of other wonders which Pisa conceals. It is worth beginning this long walk in a square, which is in itself a marvel.

■ Piazza dei Cavalieri★

This spacious, tranquil square lies in the heart of the medieval town. It has remained one of the most majestic and best-preserved areas in Pisa and it was here, in 1406, that the end of the Pisan Republic was proclaimed.

The square was totally transformed when Cosimo I de' Medici commissioned his architect, Vasari, to erect the buildings designed for the Knights of St Stephen (Cavalieri di Santo Stefano). This holy, military

Order was founded in 1562 to lead the fight against the Infidel, its main task being to capture the Muslim pirates who infested the Mediterranean. The brotherhood died out in 1860. The square is lined by 16C and 17C buildings and dominated by the **Palazzo dei Cavalieri** on which the long, unusual, slightly-curved **façade★** is decorated with grotesque figures and foliage. The upper storeys are separated by a frieze of niches containing the busts of the six members of the Medici dynasty who were Grand Dukes of Tuscany. Their coat of arms – six balls – is visible in several places, as is the Cross of the Knights who were given instruction here. The building is currently the seat of a university founded during the days of Napoleon Bonaparte. In front is a statue of Cosimo I (1596).

Palazzo dei Cavalieri

The **Church of Santo Stefano** dates from 1569 but its white, green and pink marble west front, including the Medici coat of arms and the Cross of St Stephen combined with a decoration of columns, pilasters and draperies, was built some 40 years later.

The **Palazzo dell'Orologio** (Clock House), also known as the **Gherardesca**, was reconstructed by Vasari in 1607 on the site of two older buildings. He incorporated the remains of a tower (Torre della Fame) in which, following the defeat of Pisa in 1284 at the Battle of Meloria, Count **Ugolino della Gherardesca**, the commander-in-chief of the Pisan fleet, was accused of treason and sentenced to death by starvation with his children. Dante described this episode in his *Inferno* (*Divine Comedy,* Canto XXXIII).

Walk along Via Consoli del Mare, turn left in Via Carducci, then turn right in Via S. Caterina.

▪ Santa Caterina

This church has a light **façade★** built of white marble discreetly marked with lines of darker marble. It consists of a harmonious combination of austere, wide Romanesque blind arches on the lower level and two successive rows of graceful Gothic columns and multifoiled arches on the upper sections. The interior is typical of Dominican churches, having a raftered nave but no aisles, and contains two white marble tombs facing one another – one *(left)* was sculpted by Nino Pisano in the mid-14C; the other *(right)* dates from the early 15C. The chancel is flanked by two sculptures of the *Annunciation* by Nino Pisano.

Return to Via Carducci and walk down until almost reaching the Arno.

▪ San Michele in Borgo

The **façade★** of the church is a remarkable example of the transition between the Romanesque and Gothic periods in Pisan architecture. It has three rows of galleries with trefoiled pointed arches and colonnades decorated with masks, which contrast sharply with the more robust lower section where, unlike most of the churches in Pisa, there is no blind arcading. ▪

THE LUNGARNI

■ Lungarno Mediceo

The superb **Palazzo Toscanelli** (n° 17) has a majestic Renaissance façade of pale stone and a roof projecting beyond a coffered cornice carved with roses. Byron wrote part of his *Don Juan* there between the autumn of 1821 and the summer of 1822. The **Palazzo dei Medici** (now the Prefettura) dates from the 13C-14C but has undergone much alteration since that time. Its most famous guest was Lorenzo the Magnificent of Florence.

To visit the San Matteo Museum, see the end of the tour.

■ Lungarno Pacinotti

From Piazza Solferino and the bridge of the same name, there is a view east along the **quays** of a bend in the Arno, with Monte Pisano in the background. To the west is the tall brick tower of the old citadel. The slender, white church of Santa Maria della Spina stands out on the south bank. The **Palazzo Upezzinghi** (n° 43) was built in

Gronchi Fotoarte

Detail of the
Palazzo Agostini

the early 17C and is now part of the university. Its façade flanks a large gateway, surmounted by a window opening onto a balcony, above which is a huge coat of arms decorated with a lion. The 15C **Palazzo Agostini**★ (nos 28-25) has a decorative façade built entirely of brick including two rows of Gothic windows. The frontage is covered in terracotta medallions, shields and garlands. On the ground floor is the famous **Caffè dell'Ussero** (Hussars' Café) established in 1794 and frequented by the writers of the Risorgimento. On the other side of the bridge (Ponte di Mezzo), in close proximity to each other, are the 17C **Loggia di Banchi** that used to house the linen market and the austere **Palazzo Gambacorti**, the late-14C town hall built of grey-green stone decorated with a few rows of pink stone. Its three storeys (extensively restored) include double windows set in semicircular arches.

■ Lungarno Simonelli

Along the quay rises the **Medici Arsenal**, built on the order of Cosimo I who, with his two sons Francesco I and Ferdinando I, had the ambition of turning Pisa into a maritime centre. Construction began in the mid 16C and ended in 1588.

Cross the bridge leading to the citadel.

■ San Paolo a Ripa d'Arno

As its name suggests, this 11C and 12C church stands on the bank of the Arno. Its attractive **façade**★ with three rows of columns, its alternating rows of black and white marble and the blind arcading decorating the sides are all typical of the Pisan Romanesque style and are reminiscent of the cathedral, on a less grandiose scale.

The **Cappella di Sant'Agata** behind the apse is a strange little octagonal brick chapel with a pyramid-shaped roof. It dates from the 12C and, because of its resemblance to the Church of San Sepolcro, it is usually attributed to Diotisalvi.

Continue along Lungarno Sonnino.

Façade by San Paolo a Ripa d'Arno

■ Santa Maria della Spina**

Standing alone, white and ethereal on the banks of the Arno, this tiny marble Romanesque-Gothic **church** looks like a reliquary with its spires, gables, pinnacles, niches and rose windows. For many years, it contained one of the thorns *(spina)* from Christ's Crown, hence its name.

It was built in the early 14C on a level with the river but was demolished in 1871 because of the damage caused by the proximity of the water. It was then rebuilt, stone by stone, on the spot where it stands today and underwent major restoration work, in particular on its sculptures. Several of the statues that decorated the exterior, created by the Pisano School, have been replaced by copies.

The west front includes two Romanesque doors flanked by particularly attractive delicate pink marble panels. The right side is the most ornate. It has Gothic windows, with triple or quadruple bays inserted in surbased Romanesque arches, and two doors which are also framed with coffered jambs in a style popular in the city. At the top of this wall is a row of niches containing the Redeemer and the Apostles.

The plain rectangular room forming the nave and chancel is lit, on the side facing the Arno, by an almost unbroken row of Gothic double windows beneath a Romanesque arch. The church contains a graceful *Madonna and Child* by Nino Pisano. *Proceed along the Arno.*

■ San Sepolcro

Like the Holy Sepulchre in Jerusalem, this church of the same name is built to a similar layout. Its octagonal design with pyramid-shaped roof was created in the 12C by Diotisalvi. The **interior*** consists of an ambulatory and majestic central chancel around which very tall, mighty pillars support high arches surmounted by a deep dome surrounded by brick bonding.

At the foot of the altar is the tomb of **Maria Mancini** who was removed from the French Court by her uncle, Cardinal Mazarin, because she had aroused a fierce passion in Louis XIV; she was married to Prince Colonna from whom she was later separated and who had her imprisoned. She fled to Antwerp and later to France. On being widowed she returned to Italy to spend the last few years of an unhappy life in Pisa where she died in 1715.

The tour may end with a visit of the Museo di S. Matteo. Take the Ponte alla Forteza over the Arno. ■

MUSEO NAZIONALE DI SAN MATTEO ★★

The rooms in this museum, which are set out around the cloisters in the former St Matthew's Monastery (15C), contain an extraordinary collection of sculptures and paintings, from Pisan churches and monasteries, by local artists, all showing the extent to which the city was a major centre of artistic creativity from the 13C to 15C.

■ Ground Floor

Turn right into the cloisters. The first door at the end of the gallery gives access to the collections of ceramics.

The following rooms contain ceramics imported from Liguria, southern Italy, Islamic countries or the Middle East. The collection of 10C-13C Islamic items is especially extensive.

■ First Floor

The upper gallery in the cloisters *(at the top of the staircase)* contains pieces of architectural sculpture, of which the oldest date from the 12C.

The tour of Pisan painting begins in the room on the left at the top of the staircase. The **huge Crucifixes** are characteristic of this period, which was still strongly influenced by Greek and Byzantine works. Christ is shown variously – triumphant with a calm and serene expression or suffering with his head to one side and eyes shut. Giunta di Capitinio, also known as Giunta Pisano (died mid 13C), one of the artists influenced by ancient Greek works, often accentuated the human aspect of divine suffering whereas Ranieri di Ugolino (late 13C) was representative of an innovative style based on the research carried out by Cimabue. 14C works *(right of the staircase)* show the extent to which Pisa was open to new artistic trends. The great free-standing polyptych, which is painted on one side with the glory of Saint Ursula and on the other with the glory of Saint Dominic, is by Francesco di Traino (1344). He was influenced equally by Simone Martini, a painter from Siena, and by Giotto, and painted in a mannered but vigorous style, as is evident from his *Virgin and Child with the Saints* and his *St Catherine of Alexandria* resplendent in a rich cloak *(right-hand wall)*. At the end of the room is a magnificent polyptych of the *Virgin and Child*, painted c 1320 by Simone Martini for the church of Santa Caterina; it represents (right to left) Mary Magdalen, St Dominic, St John the Evangelist, St John the Baptist, St Peter the Martyr and St Catherine; this work is attractive for the compassion in the facial expressions and is steeped in gentle melancholy.

The room at the end on the right is filled with examples of Pisan sculptures from the 14C, a period that was dominated by the workshop of Andrea Pisano and his sons, Nino (the best-known) and Tommaso. Note the delightful marble *Madonna and Child* by Nino Pisano and, more particularly, the *Madonna del latte* on which the Virgin Mary is depicted gracefully leaning over with a serene smile on her face. The work was carved jointly by Nino and his father.

The tour of the world of painting continues in the room opposite (and in the cloister gallery at right angles to it). Although the outbreak of plague in 1348 interrupted the flow of commissions and caused a break in the choice of subject matter, Pisa remained a major centre of creativity even after that date. Two of Francesco di Traino's pupils stood out from the other members of the Pisan School. They were Francesco Neri da Volterra and Cecco di Pietro. The former painted the *Madonna and Child surrounded by Saints* (to the right of the door) and the latter (against the

Ceramics

Pisa acquired a large quantity of Islamic ceramics and was also famous in the 13C-17C for its original work; from the 14C onwards production was exported throughout the Mediterranean basin from Spain to Turkey, including Provence, Corsica and Greece. It was used locally as an unusual feature in the architectural decoration of churches (see below – San Piero a Grado). From the mid-13C, Pisan workshops, which were among the largest in Tuscany, succeeded in making their ceramics waterproof by coating them in pewter-based vitreous enamels. The main feature of this "early majolica" is its brown and green painted decoration. From the 15C onwards the designs were etched into the ceramics and usually highlighted by a brown ochre tint. The item itself could be left white or uniformly painted in pale yellow, yellow ochre or green. These incisions (a stecca) later developed into the decorative style known as "peacock's feather eye".

long wall) a *Pietà* and a very ornate polyptych representing the *Crucifixion between the Saints*, whose lives are depicted on the predella.

The frescoes being painted in the Camposanto also gave painters who had learnt their craft in Florence an opportunity to work in Pisa. Among them were Spinello Aretino *(Coronation of the Virgin Mary, Three Saints)*, Agnolo Gaddi *(Four Saints)*, Taddeo di Bartolo (five charming little panels depicting the life of St Galgano) and Antonio Veneziano whose small processional pennant bears a *Crucifixion* on one side including a host of figures filled with life and vigour and, on the other, a representation of St Rainier and the Flagellants.

The following room has works by Turino Vanni (d 1444) and artists

Crucifix

Tuscan painting had strong links with Greek and Byzantine art. During the 12C a new trend developed, in Pisa and Lucca, of displaying a Crucifix in the sanctuary or in the transept crossing. There were two types of Crucifix. One showed Christ in Triumph, a hieratic and serene representation; the other depicted the Passion of Christ, his body twisted and contorted with pain. An example of the former is the Crucifix by **Berlinghieri** painted for Lucca Cathedral c 1220-30. The latter type was promoted by Giunta Pisano, who began to emphasise the pathos of Christ's Passion in the 1240's, and by the success of the sermons preached by the Franciscans, whose founder died in 1226.

Giunta adapted the Greco-Byzantine style to suit the new form of iconography, whereas **Margaritone of Arezzo** developed a degree of sensitivity and gentleness in his works, especially in the representation of St Francis himself. This trend towards Greek-style icons died out when the artists working on the decoration of the interior of the Baptistery in Florence expressed their skills in mosaics. **Cimabue**, who had worked on the enormous basilica in Assisi at the end of the 13C, showed a new approach within the traditional Byzantine forms. He succeeded in giving his figures an expressiveness that could not fail to move the congregation and induce feelings of tenderness.

influenced by him. In the centre is one of the artist's last works, a *Crucifixion* showing the donor kneeling *(left-hand side)* with the walls of Pisa behind him and the tower, already leaning *(left)*.

The other rooms reveal the level of artistic activity in Pisa in the 15C. After coming under Florentine control in 1406, Pisa saw an influx of prestigious artists from the Tuscan capital. In the corner of the cloister gallery, there is a *Virgin Mary of Humility* by Gentile da Fabriano and, in the first room in this same gallery, a *St Paul* who is amazingly lifelike. This was once part of a polyptych painted in 1426 by Masaccio, on a golden background in the Gothic tradition but in a style that was totally innovatory. There is also a *Madonna and Child* (stucco low relief) by Michelozzo, a delightful *Madonna and Child* in rather muted tones by Fra Angelico and a gilded bronze bust of St Rossore by Donatello. The following room contains a number of works by Benozzo Gozzoli and *(in the cloister gallery right)*, a *Holy Conversation* by Ghirlandaio. In the same gallery are displayed life-size sculptures in painted and gilded wood; most are by Francesco di Valdambrino who learned his craft from the Pisano family of artists; these mainly feminine figures used to decorate the convents of Pisa. ■

EXCURSIONS

THE BEACHES

30km/19mi SW of Pisa. From Pisa take the road along the south bank of the Arno and follow signs for "Mare" and "Marina di Pisa" and then for San Piero.

■ San Piero a Grado

The 11C Romanesque **basilica★** of San Piero a Grado (St Peter's on the Quay) is built of fine pale golden stone and is said to stand on the old quayside in the Roman port of Pisa where St Peter is believed to have landed. It has two apses, the one at the east end being flanked by two apsidal chapels. The Lombard arcading is decorated with alternating diamonds and circles while a frieze of ceramic bowls, a form of decoration specific to Tuscany, runs along the top of the north wall. The 14C frescoes in the interior depicting scenes from the life of St Peter are said to be copies of the ones which decorated the original basilica of St Peter's in Rome.

Tirrenia⌂ *(second turn to the right after the basilica)* is an elegant resort famous for its extensive pine woods, its white sandy beach and its film studios.

■ Marina di Pisa

It is a popular beach at the mouth of the Arno where, in spring, people fish for elvers with vast fine-mesh nets. There is a view of Livorno (south). Nearby is the vast pine wood on the **San Rossore** estate which belonged to the Medici family and then to the House of Savoy. It is now the property of the President of the Republic and part of the Migliarino-San Rossore-Massaciuccoli country park.

Take the road along the banks of the Arno to return to Pisa. ■

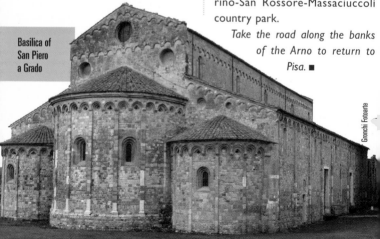

Basilica of San Piero a Grado

Gronchi Fotoarte

MONTE PISANO*

This small mountain range, an outcrop of the Apuan Alps, lying between Pisa and Lucca and separating the two cities, rises to a peak in Monte Serra.

The rugged, sheer slopes of Monte Pisano, some of which contain stone quarries, soon come into view. The narrow road lined with plane trees appproaches the mountain but remains in the plain, as if about to collide with the mountain.

■ San Giuliano Terme

This small spa town was once frequented by such famous people as Montaigne and Alfieri, and, in the 19C, by Byron, Shelley, Louis Bonaparte and Paolina Borghese. In the distance is a large yellow ochre portico with five arches.

Turn left before a small bridge to return to the village (no signs). The road runs beside a stream before crossing the first bridge on the right.

The pump rooms stand in a small square where Shelley took lodgings. The two hot springs produce water at temperatures of 38°C and 41°C. The waters of San Giuliano have been famous since Roman times and are used to treat respiratory and digestive disorders as well as arthritis and rheumatism.

60km/38mi round trip – about 2hr 30min. Leave Pisa following the north wall towards east. From Pisa take S 12 (blue signs to Lucca) and A 11 (green signs to Firenze).

Turn right opposite the pump rooms to rejoin S 12. Turn right to return to the original crossroads and turn left into the road to Calci.

At first the road runs across the arid slopes of Monte Pisano but soon the mountain becomes greener and pleasantly wooded. There are a few olive groves *(left)* and the aqueduct *(right)* which used to supply Pisa with spring water.

At the junction where the left turn leads to Agnano, Monte Pisano comes into view in the distance, sloping gently down towards the plain. The small, aptly-named "Verruca" hill, the final promontory before the descent, used to be the site of a 13C Pisan fortress which now lies in ruins. Further downhill, at the foot of one of the tower outposts of the fortress, there is a sudden break in the outline of the mountain created by the Caprona quarry which reaches right to the very edge of the fort's defences.

8km/5mi from San Giuliano, beyond a petrol station (right), turn left to Calci and Montemagno. After 1km/0.5mi of hairpin bends the road leads straight to Calci church.

■ Calci

The 11C parish church **(Pieve)** has a fine Pisan Romanesque west front. The interior underwent alterations in the 19C but has retained a font *(first chapel on the left)* used for christenings by total immersion, which dates from the second half of the 12C.

Continue along the same street. At the traffic lights go straight on (700m/ 758yd) to the charterhouse.

■ Certosa di Calci★

The Calci Charterhouse consists of an impressive set of buildings, set among olive trees on a hillside; the first stone was laid in 1366. The daily routine of the Carthusian monks alternated between their solitary cells, and the church, where they came together for worship; these buildings form part of a harmonious group, which includes the **Great Cloisters★** and the prior's lodgings.

In the 17C the Calci Charterhouse was refurbished by Giovanni Battista Cartoni (1636-51), an architect from Pisa, and Feliciano Bianchi, a monk from Siena. The fountain at the centre of the cloisters was designed by A Monzoni. In the 18C artists from Bologna such as Giuseppe and Pietro Roli and Guidi painted the frescoes in the church, artists from Carrara worked the marble on the facade and steps and Angelo Maria Somazzi from Livorno was responsible for the stuccowork.

In the 18C the buildings resounded less to the murmur of monks at prayer and more to the voices of the guests in the Grand Duke's apartment (Leopold I – Gustavus II of Sweden – Joseph II, the German Emperor – Ferdinand,

the King of Naples). The sense of abandonment is enhanced by a tour of the buildings, which passes from the pharmacy to the monks' chapels, over the paving, which has a common theme of geometric motifs in grey, black and white but varies in design from room to room; to the cemetery, past the monks' gardens to the refectory, where the name of each month (in French) appears below a figure bearing the vegetables appropriate to the season in a basket; the monks were mainly vegetarian although their rule permitted them to eat fish.

One wing of the monastery houses a **Natural History Museum**; the oldest exhibits date from the extensive collection begun by Ferdinand I of Florence in 1591. The highlight of the collection *(last floor)* is a magnificent gallery of cetaceans; the enormous skeletons contrast strangely with the view of the Charterhouse and its park which are reflected in the glass of the great showcases.

From the grounds there is a view of the surrounding mountains and the ruins of the Verruca fortress.

Return to the crossroads in Calci and turn right at the traffic lights to Monte Serra.

The road starts to climb then forms a series of narrow, hairpin bends as it mounts the slopes of Monte Pisano. After the last few houses, which are more rural in style, the road quickly enters a forest of pines and deciduous trees, alternating with stretches of heather and broom. The Arno Plain is visible *(right)* with the river winding majestically through the countryside at the foot of the mountain range. There is a superb **view★** from a lay-by *(5.3km/3mi from the crossroads in Calci).* At the Y-junction the road *(left)*

continues to climb Monte Serra, which bristles with TV masts; the other road *(right)* going down to Buti soon crosses to the opposite side of the range where the scenery becomes less rugged.

In Buti take the road to Pontedera, Lucca and Pisa; at the T-junction, opposite the river that flows through the village, turn right towards the centre. Take the first on the left and cross the bridge. Bear left; at the fork, turn left uphill. The road soon narrows and descends through a series of bends (gradient 10%/1:10) to Vicopisano (not sign-posted).

At the end of the road Vicopisano and its keep come into view on the hill.

■ Vicopisano

The Pisan Romanesque **church** (12C-13C) contains a rare wood-carving of the *Deposition from the Cross*★ (11C). The old village still has some picturesque traces of its medieval walls, including three towers – the Clock Tower, the Four Gates Tower (four pointed arches at its base) and the Brunelleschi Tower, which is connected to the keep by a machicolated wall. At the top of the hill stands the crenellated keep, next to the Palazzo Pretorio, which is decorated with a large number of coats of arms.

Take the road along the north bank of the Arno to return to Pisa.

Near **Uliveto Terme** the road skirts the rugged, rocky slopes of Monte Pisano; as it approaches Caprona, the outpost of the fortress on Verruca (visible in the distance at the start of the tour) comes into view high above a quarry which produces the yellow-ochre veined stone known as *verrucano*. ■

SAN MINIATO ★

The austere yet lively town of San Miniato retains its nobleness in its palaces, but its charm resides in two esplanades formed by the unexpected "prato" of the Dome and that of Frederick II's castle.

Its name used to be followed by the words *al Tedesco* because, from the 10C onwards, it was the official residence in Tuscany of the Holy Roman Emperors and the seat of imperial vicars. Its proud outline is broken up at the very top by the tower on the fortress and supported by the huge brick buttresses of the San Francesco Monastery, which was built on the site of the 8C San Miniato Church. A few tower-houses and palaces dating from the 15C, 16C and 17C also bear witness to a prosperous past.

Since 1947 San Miniato has been the centre of the Popular Drama Institute which stages an original dramatic work of a sacred or spiritual nature every year in July (TS Eliot, Julien Green, Thomas Mann, Elie Wiesel and Karol Wojtyla).

■ Prato del Duomo ★

The cathedral, which dates from the 12C, incorporates an older machicolated bell tower. The cathedral was altered in the 15C, 18C and

San Miniato is situated 48 km/ 30 mi on the Firenze-Pisa-Livorno motorway.

19C. It has a Romanesque façade studded with a number of 13C ceramic bowls in the Pisan tradition. The three doors date from the 15C. The **Museo Diocesano di Arte Sacra** *(left of the cathedral)* contains paintings and sculptures from the 15C-19C as well as items of sacred art.

Opposite the cathedral is the Bishop's Palace built in the 12C and initially used as the residence of the Captain of the citadel's militia. Later it was the residence of the *Signori Dodici* (the 12 magistrates of the town) and then of the Captain of the People. Since 1622 it has been the bishop's residence. The Palazzo dei Vicari dell'Imperatore (formerly the residence of the imperial vicars but now a hotel) is surmounted by a tower. It dates from the 12C and tradition has it that Countess Matilda of Tuscany was born there in 1046.

A narrow street between these two buildings leads to a tiny terrace from which there is a view of the rooftops of San Miniato and the Tuscan countryside. Below in Piazza della Repubblica is the

Two Brothers with a Love of Cinema

San Miniato is the home of **Paolo and Vittorio Taviani** (b 1929 and 1931 respectively). The brothers were inseparable and they filmed part of their work in Apulia and Sicily. They returned to their native Tuscany to film *Il Prato* (1979), shot partly in San Gimignano, *Good Morning, Babilonia* (1987) which begins in Pisa, and *La Notte di San Lorenzo* (1982) which is a reminder of a painful episode in the history of San Miniato during the Second World War.

Palazzo del Seminario★, a building with a concave façade decorated early in the 18C with frescoes and Latin aphorisms by the Fathers of the Church along the upper section; the lower part contains medieval shop fronts which have been partially preserved.

From the terrace to the left of the cathedral walk up the steep street and flight of steps (15min there and back on foot).

■ Spiazzo del Castello★
(Castle Esplanade)

The brick tower on the flattened hilltop was rebuilt so that it was identical to the original, part of Frederick II's castle *(Rocca)* which was destroyed during the last war. It is said that Pierre des Vignes, Frederick II's Chancellor, who had been accused of treason, committed suicide in the tower after his

B. Morandi/MICHELIN

eyes had been put out (Dante, *Inferno,* Song XIII).

From the esplanade there is a superb **panoramic view**★★ of San Miniato, the Arno Valley, the hills around Pisa, Pistoia and Florence, and the Appenine Mountains.

■ Santuario del Crocifisso

Behind the cathedral is the 17C **Crucifix Chapel** capped by a circular drum. The chapel contains a 10C Ottonian wooden Crucifix. A rather dramatic flight of steps leads to Via delle Vittime del Duomo.

Walk along Via delle Vittime del Duomo.

■ Palazzo Comunale

The building contains frescoes by Giotto's School, including a *Madonna and Child between the Theological Virtues* attributed to Cenni di Francesco di Ser Cenni, and a small church, Chiesa del Loretino, which has a precious altar made of marquetry with gilding and painting, a tabernacle painted by Lanfranco and 16C frescoes depicting the Life of Jesus.

Walk along Via Ser Ridolfo towards Piazza del Popolo.

■ San Domenico

This church dates from 1194 but it was altered on several occasions and its façade was never completed. One of the chapels *(on the right at the end of the nave)* contains the admirable tomb of Giovanni Chellini, the humanist doctor, attributed to Bernardo Rossellino (15C). ■

DIRECTORY

■ Transport ■

Getting There

By Air – **Galileo Galilei International Airport** (☏ 050 50 07 07) is linked to the city centre (2km/1.2mi) by the bus (15min, no 3, every 12min). There is a shuttle train between the airport and Florence (Santa Maria Novella Station, every hour).

By Train – Pisa **Central Railway Station** *(Piazza della Stazione)* is linked to Genoa (Genoa-La Spezia-Pisa line), Rome (Pisa-Livorno-Grosseto-Rome line), Lucca and Florence; change at Empoli for Siena.

By Car – Pisa is approached by road from Florence by the express route Florence-Pisa-Livorno and from north or south by the coastal motorway A 12 which runs north-south between Pisa and the sea.

Getting About

Traffic and Parking – Driving in Pisa is difficult owing to the pedestrian precincts and the one-way system designed to take traffic away from the city centre. The larger car parks are outside the town walls *(near Piazza dei Miracoli)*. There are numerous small car parks or parking spaces in the streets or along the banks of the Arno in the centre near the main sights; wait for the attendant who will issue a ticket and collect payment when you leave.

Bicycles – Rent bicycles at Pisa Scooter e Bike, or at Hotel Francesco, via S. Maria 129, ☏ 050 55 54 53, www.rental.pisa.be

■ Where to Eat ■

⊖ Budget
⊖⊖ Moderate
⊖⊖⊖ Expensive

⊖ **Osteria Dei Mille** *– Via dei Mille 32 –* ☏ *050 55 62 63 – icicapri@tin.it –* ▤ ⇔. This is a typical osteria, about 5min from the Piazza dei Miracoli, serving Tuscan cooking and a good choice of vegetarian dishes. The copper pots on the walls add a cheerful touch to the décor.

⊖ **La Clessidra** *– Via Santa Cecilia 34 –* ☏ *050 54 01 60 –* ▤ *– Reservation advised.* This simple but pleasant restaurant is in one of the most elegant and best preserved districts of Pisa. The chef will give you a taste of the typical flavours of the Tuscan region as well as one or two interesting variations of his own.

La Mescita – *V. Cavalca 2 -* ☏ *050 54 42 94 - lamescita@tin.it – Reservation advised.* In the heart of the town, with its arcades and squares, this restaurant, which has two dining-rooms, offers a calm and warm atmosphere. The chef adds his personal touch to traditional Pisan cuisine, served by an attentive staff.

Osteria dei Cavalieri – *Via San Frediano 16 –* ☏ *050 58 08 58.* This family-run trattoria, a local favourite, offers a reasonably priced menu of standard dishes served with care and a touch of originality. The warm welcome and attentive service are an added attraction.

In San Miniato

Il Convio-San Maiano – *Via San Maiano 2 - 1,5 km a sud-est -* ☏ *0571 40 81 14. This farm, outside the village, nestling in a green valley, offers a warm atmosphere and a superb view at summertime, for open air meals. Seasonal local specialities are served with great care.*

■ Where to Stay ■

☐ Budget
☐☐ Moderate
☐☐☐ Expensive

☐ **Hotel Galileo** – *Via Santa Maria 12 (1° piano senza ascensore) –* ☏ *050 40 621 – www.csinfo.it/hotelgalileo – 9 rooms €36/49.* A good address at a reasonable price in the city centre near to the Piazza dei Miracoli. The rooms have large windows and are simply furnished with modern furniture; each has its own bathroom but not en suite.

☐☐ **Hotel Amalfitana** – *Via Roma 44 –* ☏ *050 29 000 – Fax 050 25 218 –* ▤ *– 21 rooms €52/60 –* ☐ *€4.50.* A 15C mansion, a few steps from the Piazza dei Miracoli in the Santa Maria university district – could you ask for more? This a comfortable, small, family-run hotel where you will find attention to detail, courteous service and reasonable prices.

In San Miniato

☐ **Dimora del Grifo** – *V. Cesare Battisti 31 -* ☏ *0571 42 697 - Fax 0571 42 697 - dimoradelgrifo@yahoo.it -* ✉ *- 5 cam.* A simple yet neat solution for those who wish to stay in San Miniato. Basic lodging and shared bathrooms

■ Taking a Break ■

Caffè dell'Ussero – *Lungarno Pacinotti 27 –* ☏ *050 58 11 00 – Open Sun-Fri, 7.30am-9pm; closed Aug.* This café, founded in 1794, is situated beside the Arno on the ground floor of the Palazzo Rosso. First it was frequented by intellectuals, then it became a musical café and then a cinema; now it is a cosy tea room.

Pasticceria Federico Salza – *Borgo Stretto 46 –* ☎ *050 58 02 44 - info@salza.it – Open 7am-8pm; Easter-Aug closed Mon.* This café is divided into a cosy bar and a large and light tea room. Its charming terrace under the arches looking onto a picturesque street attracts many customers

■ Shopping ■

In San Miniato

Il Cantuccio di Federigo *– V. P. Maioli 67 -* ☎ *0571 41 83 44 - paolo. gazzarrini@libero.it.* Paolo Gazzari's special care in choosing pastries and wines makes it quite a unique place. Despite its established renown, Il cantuccio di Federigo remains a place where the flavour of simple and traditional food products can still be found.

■ Events and Festivals ■

See the section "Pisan Festivals".

In San Miniato

Ancient traditions are still celebrated today. For instance, during the Feast of St John (Fuochi di San Giovanni), which takes place on the shortest day of the year, bonfires are lit and corncobs and cloves of garlic are burnt on the surrounding hills, to ward off bad luck. In these hills grow **white truffles** which are picked in Autumn. These precious mushrooms are the object of a great fair taking place on the last three weekends in November.

INDEX

Director	David Brabis
Series Editor	Manuela Magni
Editorial Team	Erica Zane, Elisabetta Rossi, Sybille Bouquet, Aude de La Coste-Messelière, Juliette Hubert, Pierre Boussard, Élise Pinsolle
Picture Editor	Catherine Guégan
Mapping	Michèle Cana, Thierry Lemasson
Graphics Coordination	Marie-Pierre Renier
Graphics	Antoine Diemoz-Rosset
Lay-out	Michel Moulin
Typesetting	Sophie Rassel et Franck Malagie (NORD COMPO)
Production	Renaud Leblanc
Marketing	Agathe Mérel
Sales	Paolo Riccardi
Public Relations	Kenol Verdoia

Special Thanks: GRONCHI FOTOARTE, Pisa; Alessandro Canestrelli, Agenzia per il Turismo di Pisa; Giuseppe Settembrini

Contact Michelin – Edizioni per Viaggiare
Via Vincenzo Monti, 23
20016 PERO (MI)
☎ 02 33 95 35 41 – fax 02 33 95 37 38
www.ViaMichelin.it
LaGuidaVerde@it.michelin.com

Edizioni per Viaggiare

Michelin Italiana S.p.A.
Via V. Monti, 23 – 20016 PERO
www.ViaMichelin.it
LaGuidaVerde@it.michelin.com

MANUFACTURE FRANÇAISE DES PNEUMATIQUES MICHELIN
Société en commandite par actions au capital de 304 000 000 EUR
Place des Carmes-Déchaux – 63 Clermont-Ferrand (France)
R.C.S. Clermont-Fd B 855 200 507

Published in 2004

Front cover: *The Leaning tower, detail* (B. Pérousse/MICHELIN) – *Duomo* (G. Settembrini/MICHELIN) – *Detail of a fresco, Camposanto* (Ph. Orain/MICHELIN) – *Leaning tower* (G. Settembrini/MICHELIN) – *Palazzo dei Cavalieri, detail* (G. Settembrini/MICHELIN) – *Lungarno Pacinotti* (G. Settembrini/MICHELIN)